What Others Are Saying About This Book …

"Thrive and Lead is a must-have for every woman looking to step into her power and lead her best life! If you're looking to create a thriving business balanced with an extraordinary personal life, DJ Neyhart will get you there. The unique 'inside-out' approach lays down the building blocks with foundational mindset tips combined with practical 'how to' steps, all laid out in an easy-to-read intimate experience."

- **Cindy Watson** USA Today best-selling author of
The Art of Feminine Negotiation
www.ArtOfFeminineNegociation.com

"Dj's compassionate wisdom flows through the pages of this wonderfully practical guide. If you're ready for the next step and would benefit from some excellent support, read this book!"

- **Lexie Bebbington**, CPCC, www.LexieBebbington.co.uk

"This book is a treasure trove of strategic insights and heartfelt advice, guiding women entrepreneurs through the trials and triumphs of building a business."

- **Barb Smith**, Caregiver Coach, www.SereneCaregiving.com

"Every chapter of 'Thrive and Lead' resonates with authenticity and practical wisdom, making it an indispensable guide for women entrepreneurs everywhere."

- **Jill Clair**, Business Coach, www.JillClair.com

"DJ Neyhart's compelling narrative and actionable advice make "Thrive & Lead" stand out for its depth, practicality, and ability to connect with women at all stages of their careers." - **Klara Gallusz**, Business Coach

"'Thrive & Lead' is the companion every female entrepreneur needs to stay inspired, overcome obstacles, and succeed in the competitive business world."

- **Christiana Gill**, Business Coach, www.CMGPremiere.com

"From cover to cover, 'Thrive & Lead' is a masterclass in business acumen fused with personal development, tailored specifically for women looking to lead with strength and grace."

- **Linda Kattan**, Coach, www.ResetYourGPSforSuccess.com

Thrive and Lead

Thrive and Lead

Balancing Success and Fulfillment for Women Entrepreneurs

DJ Neyhart

CHANGE YOUR
FUTURE
PUBLISHING

Thrive and Lead
Balancing Success and Fulfillment for Women Entrepreneurs
By DJ Neyhart
Published by Change Your Future Publishing

Author's Note:
Go to www.ThriveAndLeadBonuses.com for more information, tips, resources and strategies designed to help you in your journey to success.

Disclaimer:
The information contained in this book is for general informational purposes only. The views expressed in this book are those of the author and do not necessarily reflect the views of the publisher. While the author has made every effort to ensure the accuracy and completeness of the information presented, the author and publisher assume no responsibility for errors, inaccuracies, omissions, or any other inconsistencies herein.

The advice and strategies contained herein may not be suitable for every situation. This book is sold with the understanding that the author and publisher are not engaged in rendering legal, accounting, medical, or other professional services. Readers should seek professional advice for their specific situation.

The author and publisher shall not be liable for any loss, damage, or injury, including but not limited to special, incidental, consequential, or other damages, caused or alleged to have been caused directly or indirectly by the information contained in this book.

Copyright © 2024, DJ Neyhart, All Rights Reserved.

No part of this book may be reproduced in any form or by any electronic or mechanical means, including information storage and retrieval systems, without permission in writing from the publisher, except by a reviewer who may quote brief passages in a review.

If you find any typographical errors in this book, they are there for a reason. Some people love looking for them and we strive to please as many people as possible.

ISBN: 9798334604575
First Edition, 2024
Printed in the United States of America
10 9 8 7 6 5 4 3 2 1

To all the beautiful women across the globe who have ever doubted their worth or questioned their ability to be amazing, strong, confident, healthy, and wealthy business entrepreneurs: this book is for you. You possess more strength and power than you could possibly imagine. May this work inspire you, may your hopes and dreams be realized, and may you transform them into your ultimate reality. Stand tall, forge ahead, and never forget that you are more than enough.

Contents

Introduction		1
Chapter 1	Visionary Beginnings	7
Chapter 2	Strategic Movements	14
Chapter 3	Mindset for Success	20
Chapter 4	Skill Enhancement	29
Chapter 5	Optimizing Your Environment	36
Chapter 6	Mastering Work-Life Integration	42
Chapter 7	Building and Leveraging Networks	47
Chapter 8	Financial Planning for the Future	53
Chapter 9	Leadership and Empowerment	58
Chapter 10	Sustaining Growth and Pursuing New Horizons	66
Conclusion		71
Next Steps		77

Acknowledgements

Writing this book has been a journey of reflection, growth, and gratitude. As I share these words, my heart is filled with immense appreciation for those who have supported, encouraged, and believed in me along the way.

First and foremost, I would like to extend my deepest thanks to Christian Mickelsen, Barbara Smith, Jill Clair, Klara Gallusz, and the entire team at Future Force, Inc. Each of you has played a pivotal role in my development, allowing me to blossom both personally and professionally. Your guidance has not only nurtured my growth but also revealed to me my true warrior potential. Your encouragement and support have been instrumental in my journey.

I must also express my profound gratitude to my mother, Sheri, whose spirit and support continue to guide me, even in her absence. Mom, your love and belief in my capabilities remain a cornerstone of my strength. Your support will forever be cherished and never go unappreciated.

To my fabulous family—Cyndi, Nick, Alonna, Ally, Jarrod, and Judy—thank you for your unwavering support, love, and patience. Each of you has contributed to my life in invaluable ways, supporting me tirelessly as I pursued my dreams. Your endless encouragement and understanding have been my anchor.

A special thanks to all my friends and colleagues, and to Andy, whose understanding and support have been steadfast. Your presence and encouragement have been a source of comfort and motivation, helping me to navigate the challenges and celebrate the victories.

And how could I forget my six loving fur babies? Thank you for your endless affection, loyalty, companionship, and the sheer cuteness that brightens my days. You bring joy and light-heartedness into my daily life, reminding me of the simple pleasures that life has to offer.

To all of you who have been part of this incredible journey, your support has not only made this book possible but has profoundly shaped the person I am today. Thank you from the bottom of my heart.

Introduction

Welcome to "Thrive and Lead: Balancing Success and Fulfillment for Women Entrepreneurs," a book crafted for women who dare to dream of owning a thriving business while enjoying a fulfilling personal life. This book is your companion in carving out a path that harmonizes your entrepreneurial ambitions with your personal aspirations, ensuring that you don't have to sacrifice one for the other.

As an entrepreneur, a mother, and someone who has navigated the rough tides of health challenges and business environments alike, I've lived the very stories and strategies I share with you. Over the years, I've learned that true success is not just about financial gains or business growth; it's also about leading a life that brings you joy and satisfaction on all fronts.

Women entrepreneurs often feel the pressure to do everything on their own, juggling countless responsibilities while trying to excel in both their personal and professional lives. However, you don't have to navigate this journey alone. By relying on others and fostering connections, you can create a more balanced and abundant life, ultimately enhancing both your personal and business experiences.

Women entrepreneurs face a unique set of challenges. The business world, historically male-dominated, often sets standards and expectations that do not take the complex lives of women into account. Many women feel the pressure to choose between pursuing a career and investing in their personal lives. However, the landscape is changing. More and more women are taking the helm of their own businesses, demonstrating that it is possible to be both a successful entrepreneur and a dedicated parent, partner, or friend.

This book unfolds the five basic steps to building a business, providing a blueprint for you to follow. But it's not just about the nuts and bolts of business planning and execution. It's about weaving these with the threads of your life to create a tapestry that is as rewarding as it is beautiful. Here's what we'll explore together:

First, the power of vision. Your business starts with a vision. This isn't just any vision, but one that clearly aligns with who you are and what you value most. When I started my journey, having a clear vision helped me navigate through the toughest times, especially when I was juggling my health issues with the demands of starting a new business. Your vision will be the beacon that keeps you focused and directed as you steer your business through ups and downs.

Second, we'll talk about strategy. Having a great vision without a strategy is like having a destination without a map. A well-crafted strategy will guide your daily actions and decisions, helping you to manage your resources effectively and keep your business on track. From my own experience, I know that a good strategy considers not just business growth, but also personal well-being. It's about finding the best route that serves both your professional objectives and personal needs.

Third, your mindset. The right mindset can be your greatest asset or your biggest barrier. Throughout this book, I share stories of how overcoming doubts and fostering a positive, resilient mindset propelled me forward. Whether it was pushing through after my 23rd surgery or tackling the next big business challenge, maintaining a healthy mindset was crucial.

Fourth, we'll focus on skills. The landscape of business is ever-evolving, and staying equipped with the right skills is imperative. This book doesn't just list the skills you need; it shows you how and where to acquire them. Sometimes, it's through formal education, and other times, it's through life's unexpected lessons. I've enhanced my abilities through both, and I'll guide you on how to do the same.

Finally, your environment. Creating an environment that nurtures your growth is essential. This means setting up physical spaces that foster productivity and cultivating relationships that support your endeavors. When I established a dedicated workspace at home, it was a game-changer, and so was having a supportive community around me.

But this book is more than just a guide to starting and running a business; it's a manifesto for living a life that you love. It's about making your entrepreneurial journey one of joy, growth, and balance. Through the chapters, you'll find practical steps intertwined with insights from my own life—how I managed a business while being a mom to three wonderful children and a host of fur babies, and how I've built networks that not only supported my business but also enriched my personal life.

Why is this important for women entrepreneurs today? Because you are part of a powerful shift in the business world. More than ever, women are creating and leading companies that are not only profitable but also transformative. You are not just building businesses; you are creating opportunities for yourself and others, setting new standards, and breaking old barriers.

As we move through this book together, I invite you to think of it as a conversation between friends, one where I share what I've learned in the hope that it helps you on your journey. Whether you're just starting out or looking to take your business to the next level, remember, you have the power to shape your life and your business into something truly remarkable.

This is your time to thrive and lead, to show the world not just what women entrepreneurs are capable of, but what they can redefine success to look like. Let's begin this adventure together, and let's make it one for the books!

"You are never too old to set another goal or to dream a new dream." C.S Lewis

Chapter 1
Visionary Beginnings

Creating a clear vision is perhaps the most crucial step you can take as an entrepreneur. It's like setting up the foundations of a house—the stronger and clearer the foundation, the sturdier and more reliable the house will be. A clear vision in entrepreneurship acts as a guiding star, helping to navigate through the uncertainties of business and aligning your daily actions with your long-term objectives.

The Importance of a Clear Vision in Entrepreneurship

A clear vision serves multiple vital purposes. It not only sets the direction and defines the destination but also motivates and inspires both you and those around you. Imagine setting off on a journey without knowing your destination. You might wander aimlessly, encounter numerous unnecessary challenges, and waste resources. The same can happen in business without a clear vision.

This vision is not just a fleeting thought or a daydream. It's a vivid, detailed picture of what you want your future to look like. It encompasses both your personal and professional aspirations, reflecting your deepest values and highest ambitions. As Tony Robbins once said, "Setting goals is the first step in turning the invisible into the visible." This is especially true for your vision—it transforms intangible ideas into tangible goals.

Mapping Out Your Business and Personal Goals

Creating a detailed vision involves deep reflection and foresight, requiring you to look not just days or months ahead, but years into your future. Start with your long-term goals: where do you see yourself in five years? What kind of life do you want to lead? What kind of business do you want to run? These questions set the stage for more detailed planning.

Once you have a clear picture of your five-year goals, break them down further into three-year and two-year milestones. This approach helps you build a bridge between your current position and your long-term vision. From there, distill these milestones into one-year goals, which can be broken down even further into six-month and monthly goals. Finally, think about what you need to do in the next 30 days, and even in the next week, to set yourself on the right path.

For each timeframe, your goals should be specific, measurable, achievable, relevant, and time-bound (SMART). This level of detail adds clarity and urgency, turning your vision into a step-by-step action plan. For instance, if your five-year goal is to run a multi-million dollar business, your three-year goal might be to hit the half-million mark. To achieve that, your two-year goal could involve expanding your product line or customer base. Breaking it down by year, you might focus on building your brand identity or improving your online presence.

When I started my journey, my initial vision was rather basic —simply to be my own boss and make enough money to support my family. However, as I delved deeper into the planning process, I realized the importance of having a more detailed vision. It wasn't just about sustaining my family anymore; it was about creating a thriving business that could also bring personal fulfillment and allow for growth both for myself and those I worked with.

I wanted to dream big—not just in terms of financial success but in what my business could contribute to the community and how it could reflect my personal values. This broader, more exciting vision became a powerful motivator. It wasn't just a plan; it was a dream that I was eager to turn into reality.

Implementing Your Vision

Putting your vision into action involves regular reviews and adjustments. Life is unpredictable, and flexibility is crucial. As your business grows and evolves, so too might your personal circumstances. Your vision should grow and adapt with you. This adaptability was crucial for me as I navigated the challenges of balancing business growth with personal health issues and family commitments.

In the early days, it was particularly challenging to see the bigger picture when the day-to-day responsibilities seemed overwhelming. However, by keeping my detailed vision in mind and regularly revisiting and revising my plans, I was able to steer my business and personal life in the direction I truly wanted them to go.

There was a time in my life when the future seemed particularly uncertain. After surviving over 23 surgeries, each day felt like a battle, and I was left wondering where to go from there. My professional life as the Vice President of a small consulting firm had been fulfilling, but as my health deteriorated, I found myself unable to maintain the responsibilities my role demanded. It was during this tumultuous period that I realized I needed to pause and reassess not just my career, but my overall direction in life.

The turning point came when I began to ask myself some fundamental questions: What did I really want from my life? Where did I see myself heading? This reflection led me to realize the importance of having a clear and compelling vision. I needed to visualize a future where I could thrive despite the challenges I faced. Through this process, I gained clarity about shifting my career towards something more manageable and profoundly impactful—becoming a coach.

Today, I live a fulfilling life, guiding others on how to balance success and personal fulfillment, teaching them to "Thrive and Lead." My journey from a high-powered executive to a board certified coach wasn't just about changing professions—it was about transforming my life through the power of vision. This path of rediscovery was not easy, but as Joel A. Barker famously said, "Vision without action is merely a dream. Action without vision just passes the time. Vision with action can change the world."

This story is a testament to the power of having a vision. It's not merely about professional aspirations; it's also about personal rebirth and resilience. If I had not taken the time to define what I truly wanted, to crystallize that vision and move toward it, I might not have found the strength to rebuild my life and career on my own terms. Let this serve as an encouragement to you: no matter where you are in your journey, take the time to understand and define your vision. It is the first, most crucial step towards achieving not just business success, but a balanced and fulfilling life.

A clear and detailed vision is not just a tool for strategic planning—it's a source of motivation and inspiration. It aligns your daily actions with your long-term goals and helps keep you on track through the ups and downs of entrepreneurship. By dreaming big and mapping out your goals with precision, you can turn the vision of your ideal business and personal life into a tangible reality. Just remember, the more detailed your vision, the clearer your path to success will be. As you embark on this journey, take to heart the words of C.S. Lewis: "You are never too old to set another goal or to dream a new dream." This is your entrepreneurial journey, shaped by your dreams and driven by your actions.

"It is not enough to be busy... The question is: what are we busy about?" Henry David Thoreau

Chapter 2

Strategic Movements

Once you have established a clear vision for your business and personal life, the next crucial step is to develop a strategy that aligns with this vision. A strategy is your roadmap; it lays out how you intend to reach your destination. Without a strategic plan, even the clearest vision can become like a ship without a rudder, drifting aimlessly and vulnerable to the currents of everyday challenges and distractions.

The Necessity of Having a Strategy Aligned with Your Vision

Imagine embarking on a journey to a new and exciting destination. You wouldn't start driving without a map or directions; otherwise, you would waste fuel, time, and effort, and still might not reach where you want to go. Similarly, in business and life, a strategy ensures that every effort you make moves you closer to your vision. It helps you allocate resources efficiently, make decisions under pressure, and stay on track amidst distractions and competing priorities.

A strategy aligned with your vision also ensures consistency in your actions and decisions. This alignment helps maintain focus, especially when faced with opportunities or challenges that might lead you astray. For every decision, you can ask yourself: Does this align with my vision? Is this part of my strategy? This approach helps filter out what is essential and what is not, keeping you on the path to your goals.

Steps to Develop and Implement Effective Business Strategies

Developing and implementing an effective business strategy involves several key steps:

1. **Break Down Your Vision into Objectives**: Start by translating your overarching vision into specific, measurable objectives. If your vision includes growing your business into a certain market, your objectives might involve reaching specific sales targets or expanding your customer base.

2. **Analyze Your Resources and Capabilities**: Understand what resources you have available and what capabilities you need to develop. This analysis will help you identify gaps in your skills, knowledge, or finances that need to be addressed to achieve your objectives.

3. **Create Actionable Steps**: Convert your objectives into actionable steps. This means setting smaller goals that lead to the completion of your larger objectives. Each goal should have a clear timeline and defined metrics for success.

4. **Prioritize Your Actions**: Not all actions are of equal importance. Prioritize tasks based on their impact on your objectives and the resources they require. Start with

actions that will have the most significant immediate impact on your goals.

5. **Implement the Plan**: Put your strategy into action. This involves not just doing the work but also monitoring your progress and making adjustments as needed. Regular check-ins on your strategy's effectiveness are crucial.

6. **Evaluate and Adjust**: The business world is dynamic, so flexibility is key. Regularly evaluate your strategy against your actual progress and current market conditions. Be prepared to make adjustments to stay aligned with your vision.

In my own journey, I learned the hard way that without prioritization, even the best strategies can fall apart. I used to end each day wondering where my time went. Despite having a comprehensive list of tasks, I found myself continuously distracted by phone calls, household chores, and other immediate but less important demands.

It was a conversation with my personal coach that turned things around. I learned to focus on the top three items on my daily list before considering anything else. This focus was transformational. As J.R.R. Tolkien wisely noted, "All we have to decide is what to do with the time that is given us." I chose to prioritize tasks that directly impacted my goals, and suddenly, I was making real progress.

By mapping out how I was going to achieve my goals, it made it much easier to prioritize and accomplish my daily goals.

Making Daily Lists and Prioritizing Key Tasks

To effectively implement this in your daily life, start each day by writing a list of tasks. Then, identify the top three tasks that will most effectively propel you towards your goals. Commit to completing these before moving on to less critical tasks. This method ensures that even on days when not everything gets done, the most impactful tasks are completed, keeping you aligned with your strategic path.

This chapter lays out the framework for transforming your vision into a tangible strategy and the daily habits that will help you implement this strategy effectively. With these tools, you are well on your way to making your vision a reality, strategically navigating through the complexities of business and personal life with confidence and focus.

"You must master a new way to think before you can master a new way to be." Marianne Williamson

Chapter 3
Mindset for Success

The journey to success in both business and personal life is significantly influenced by one's mindset. The way you think shapes your perceptions, your actions, and ultimately, the outcomes you achieve. It is crucial, therefore, to cultivate a mindset that not only encourages positive thinking but also supports action-oriented steps towards your goals. This chapter will delve into the essential role that mindset plays in achieving success and offer techniques to foster a mindset that propels you forward rather than holding you back.

The Role of Mindset in Achieving Business and Personal Success

Mindset is the lens through which we view our world, challenges, and opportunities. It affects every decision we make and every interaction we have. For entrepreneurs, a positive, growth-oriented mindset is indispensable. It's not just about thinking positively but about being resilient and adaptable in the face of challenges and failures. As Henry Ford famously said, "Whether you think you can, or you think you can't – you're right." This statement underscores the power of mindset in shaping our reality.

A positive mindset leads to more than just occasional good feelings—it directly impacts your effectiveness as a leader and entrepreneur. It fosters an environment where creativity and innovation can flourish, and where resilience becomes the norm. With a strong, positive mindset, obstacles become merely temporary setbacks that provide learning opportunities rather than insurmountable barriers.

Techniques for Overcoming Doubts and Fostering a Positive Mindset

Cultivating a positive mindset often requires us to confront and overcome our deepest doubts and fears. These negative beliefs can be deeply ingrained, and they typically manifest as doubts about our abilities, the value of our work, or our worthiness of success. Overcoming these doubts is crucial because they can stifle growth and prevent us from taking the actions necessary to achieve our goals.

1. **Awareness and Acknowledgment**: The first step to changing your mindset is to become aware of your negative thoughts and beliefs. Acknowledge these thoughts without judgment. Understanding that these are merely thoughts, not facts, can help you distance yourself from them.

2. **Reframing Thoughts**: Once you recognize a negative thought, actively reframe it into a positive or neutral statement. For example, change "I can't do this" to "I haven't done this yet, but I can learn." This technique shifts your focus from perceived limitations to potential growth.

3. **Visualization**: Visualize yourself achieving your goals. This technique is powerful because the brain often does not distinguish between real and vividly imagined experiences. Regular visualization can enhance motivation and reinforce your belief in your ability to succeed.

4. **Mindfulness and Meditation**: These practices help in managing stress and reducing anxiety, which are often the sources of negative thinking. By becoming more mindful, you can learn to remain present and focused, rather than being overwhelmed by future fears or past regrets.

5. **Seek Support**: Sometimes, the best way to shift your mindset is to lean on others for support. This could be a mentor, coach, or even a supportive peer group. These individuals can provide encouragement, offer new perspectives, and help you navigate through your mental blocks.

For instance, consider the story of my client, Debbie. Debbie's intelligence, creativity, and knowledge in her field were beyond question, but her business struggled to take off for years. The root cause was not a lack of business acumen but her mindset. Debbie was plagued by doubts: Am I good enough? What if I fail? What will people think of me? Can I really charge money for my services? These doubts crippled her ability to move forward.

When we began working together, we focused intensely on transforming her mindset. Through various techniques, including the ones listed above, Debbie learned to release the emotions and beliefs that were not serving her. The transformation was remarkable. Not only did her business begin to thrive, but her personal life also improved significantly. She started working fewer hours, earning more, and spending more quality time with her family.

This transformation highlights a vital point: "You must master a new way to think before you can master a new way to be," as Marianne Williamson puts it. Changing your mindset isn't just about feeling better; it's about creating a foundation that allows you to act differently and achieve outcomes you once thought were out of reach.

In the realm of maintaining a positive mindset and overcoming doubts, it is crucial to address not only the mental hurdles related to your business endeavors but also personal challenges that can significantly impact your overall well-being and performance. A compelling illustration of this is the story of one of my clients, Cyndi, who approached me during a particularly stressful time in her life.

Cyndi was struggling with severe anxiety stemming from a recurring nightmare, which significantly disrupted her sleep. This lack of rest was hindering her ability to complete day-to-day tasks and was exacerbating her anxiety, creating a vicious cycle that she felt powerless to escape. Understandably, this situation was taking a toll on both her personal life and her business operations.

When Cyndi came to me for help, we spent about thirty minutes working through her concerns and implementing techniques designed to manage her anxiety and alter her mindset about sleep. The results were immediate and profound. Cyndi reported a significant decrease in her anxiety levels and felt a renewed sense of calm about going to sleep that evening. I am elated to report that after our session, Cyndi experienced a peaceful night's sleep and has not encountered the same issues since. Just being able to sleep without the dread of her recurring nightmare lifted a huge weight off her shoulders, enabling her to move forward with her life more positively and productively.

This story underscores the importance of addressing all aspects of one's mental health to maintain a strong, positive mindset. By managing personal challenges like Cyndi's, the pathways clear for not only improved personal well-being but also enhanced professional performance. Let this serve as a reminder of the transformative power of confronting and overcoming personal barriers, which in turn can catalyze profound professional success and personal fulfillment.

As we discuss the significance of maintaining a positive mindset and overcoming doubts, it is important to also consider the physical aspects that can significantly impact our mental and physical performance. Integrating simple health practices into your daily routine can bolster your mental clarity and overall well-being, which are essential for sustained success.

If you work sitting down, like most of us do, it's crucial to be mindful of your physical health while managing your mental space. An effective strategy is to stand up every hour, or at least every two hours, and take a moment to shake your body out and move around. This simple activity helps keep your blood circulating effectively and ensures that your lymphatic system functions efficiently. These small physical breaks can greatly reduce the lethargy and discomfort that often come with prolonged sitting, enhancing your ability to stay focused and productive.

Additionally, staying hydrated is another key element that supports both mental and physical health. Make sure to drink plenty of water or other low-sugar liquids throughout the day. Hydration aids in maintaining optimal brain function and energy levels, both of which are crucial for tackling the challenges and tasks that come with running a business and leading a team.

Implementing these small, health-focused practices into your daily work routine can lead to significant improvements in your overall health, ultimately contributing to your mental and physical success. Remember, taking care of your body is just as important as nurturing your mind when it comes to achieving and maintaining peak performance in business and life.

> Your mindset is not just a small component of your entrepreneurial journey; it is the bedrock upon which all your endeavors rest. By cultivating a positive, growth-oriented mindset, you set the stage not only for business success but also for a fulfilling and enriching personal life. Remember, the mind is a powerful thing. What you think, you become. What you feel, you attract. What you imagine, you create.

"Live as if you were to die tomorrow. Learn as if you were to live forever." Mahatma Gandhi

Chapter 4
Skill Enhancement

The business landscape is dynamic and ever-evolving. To stay relevant and competitive, continuously upgrading your skills is not just beneficial—it's essential. This chapter delves into why it's crucial to keep your skills sharp and how to effectively foster continual learning and development to ensure both you and your business do not just survive but thrive.

The Importance of Continually Upgrading Your Skills

In today's fast-paced world, new technologies, methodologies, and best practices emerge at a breakneck pace. The skills that were in demand yesterday might be obsolete tomorrow. Continually upgrading your skills ensures that you can adapt to changes and capitalize on new opportunities as they arise. As Alvin Toffler famously said, "The illiterate of the 21st century will not be those who cannot read and write, but those who cannot learn, unlearn, and relearn." This ability to learn, unlearn, and relearn is what keeps you and your business agile and forward-thinking.

For entrepreneurs, staying updated with skills is not just about personal growth. It's about ensuring your business processes, products, and services remain top-notch. It involves understanding market trends, adapting to new technologies, and improving customer engagement strategies. Every new skill you acquire can open up additional avenues for business development and growth.

Moreover, upgrading your skills can lead to better decision-making. With a broader knowledge base, you can foresee potential challenges and opportunities, making strategic decisions that can lead your business to new heights. It also sets a precedent for your team, cultivating a culture of learning and adaptation within your organization.

Resources and Methods for Skill Development

There are numerous resources and methods available today that make learning new skills accessible to everyone. Here are some effective ways to continue your education and skill development:

1. **Online Courses**: Platforms like Coursera, Udemy, and LinkedIn Learning offer a wide array of courses taught by industry experts. Whether it's digital marketing, coding, or financial management, there's likely a course that fits your needs. These platforms allow you to learn at your own pace, fitting education into your busy schedule.

2. **Books and eBooks**: Never underestimate the power of a good book. Many experts share their knowledge through writing. Books not only provide deep insights into various subjects but also expose you to new perspectives and ideas. Whether it's a classic business book or the latest publication on startup strategies, reading regularly is a fantastic way to enhance your skills.

3. **Workshops and Seminars**: Attending workshops and seminars is a great way to learn new skills and network

with other professionals. These are particularly useful for hands-on learning and can provide a more interactive environment to discuss ideas and strategies with peers and experts.

4. **Webinars and Podcasts**: With the digital age in full swing, learning has transcended traditional boundaries. Webinars and podcasts can be an excellent way to gain insights from industry leaders without the need to travel. They can provide valuable tips and strategies and keep you updated on the latest industry trends.

5. **Mentorship and Coaching**: Sometimes, personalized guidance is what you need to take your skills to the next level. Finding a mentor or hiring a coach can provide you with tailored advice and feedback that is specific to your industry and challenges.

In my experience, even when it comes to tasks like hiring new team members, it's crucial to have the right skills to identify the best candidates. Recognizing the signs of a great employee goes beyond their resume; it involves understanding their behavior, assessing cultural fit, and predicting their potential impact on your team. Taking a short course on modern hiring practices or interviewing techniques can be immensely beneficial and ensure you make informed hiring decisions.

For instance, learning to read non-verbal cues or understanding personality assessments can transform your approach to interviews and help you choose candidates who not only have the right skills but also align with your company's values and culture.

After establishing a clear vision and strategic implementation plan, and dedicating considerable effort to getting my mindset right, I recognized the need to advance my skill set to effectively run my coaching business. This realization marked the beginning of a rigorous learning journey.

I wasn't naturally tech-savvy, which posed a significant challenge initially as technology is integral to running a modern business, especially one in coaching that relies heavily on digital communication and marketing tools. To bridge this gap, I immersed myself in numerous educational opportunities. I attended a variety of workshops that offered hands-on experience, participated in webinars that I could attend from the comfort of my home, and enrolled in several courses that were focused on enhancing technological skills.

Additionally, I read a multitude of books that not only inspired me but also gave practical advice on various business technologies.

Each step in this journey of skill enhancement was aimed at building a robust foundation for my coaching business. The effort to update and refine my abilities was intense and at times overwhelming, but profoundly rewarding. This phase of skill development was crucial; it transformed me from someone who merely had a vision into someone capable of executing that vision effectively.

Through this personal experience, I learned that being open to acquiring new skills—regardless of how daunting they might seem at the outset—is essential for any entrepreneur. It's not just about personal growth but ensuring that your business can thrive in a competitive environment. As you continue to learn and adapt, remember that each new skill you acquire not only brings you closer to your business goals but also enhances your confidence as a leader and innovator.

Continually upgrading your skills is a critical component of maintaining a competitive edge in business. It allows you to adapt to changes, meet challenges head-on, and seize opportunities that come your way. As Mahatma Gandhi once said, "Live as if you were to die tomorrow. Learn as if you were to live forever." This philosophy is especially pertinent for entrepreneurs. The commitment to lifelong learning is what will keep you relevant, resilient, and ready to lead your business toward continued success.

"We shape our dwellings, and afterwards our dwellings shape us." Winston Churchill

Chapter 5
Optimizing Your Environment

Creating a productive and supportive work environment is crucial for any entrepreneur, especially for those who operate from home. The challenge of maintaining a clear distinction between personal and professional life can be substantial without the physical separation that a traditional office provides. However, with the right strategies and mindset, you can transform your home into a space that fosters both efficiency and creativity.

Creating a Productive and Supportive Work Environment

A productive work environment is one that promotes efficiency and minimizes stress. This goes beyond just physical space—it encompasses the atmosphere, the culture, and the practices that you establish. It's about creating an environment where you can focus deeply and produce your best work. As Steve Jobs famously said, "The only way to do great work is to love what you do." Ensuring that your workspace is conducive to this love and dedication is essential.

Firstly, it's important to cultivate an atmosphere of professionalism, even at home. This means having a dedicated workspace that is free from personal clutter and distractions. Your workspace should signal to your brain that it's time for work, not relaxation. This separation helps in mentally preparing you for productive work and creates a psychological boundary that can help manage work-life balance.

Tips for Setting Up a Home Office That Fosters Efficiency and Creativity

When setting up a home office, consider the following tips to ensure it enhances your productivity and sparks your creativity:

1. **Choose the Right Location**: Ideally, your office should be in a quiet area of your home where distractions are minimized. If possible, use a room with a door you can close to separate yourself physically and mentally from the rest of your household activities.

2. **Invest in Comfortable and Functional Furniture**: Your desk and chair are the most critical pieces of furniture in your office. Choose ergonomically designed options that support your posture and comfort for long hours of work. Comfort in your physical workspace boosts productivity and helps prevent fatigue and physical strain.

3. **Good Lighting is Key**: Natural light is best for both your eyesight and your overall well-being. Set up your workspace to maximize exposure to natural light. If that's not possible, invest in proper artificial lighting that

brightens your workspace without causing glare or harsh shadows.

4. **Minimize Distractions**: Keep your workspace tidy and organized. Clutter can lead to mental clutter, which impedes creativity and efficiency. Also, manage technological distractions by keeping your mobile phone out of sight during work hours or using apps that limit your access to distracting websites.

5. **Personalize Your Space**: Adding personal touches such as plants, artwork, or motivational quotes can make your workspace feel welcoming and stimulating. These elements can boost your mood and creativity, making your office a place you enjoy spending time in.

In my experience, setting clear boundaries was a game-changer. Initially, working from home was more challenging than anticipated due to constant interruptions. It wasn't until I established specific work hours and communicated these boundaries to my family that I saw a significant decrease in disruptions. I made it clear when I was available and when I was not to be disturbed unless it was urgent. I also set similar expectations with my team, who knew my schedule and understood how to reach me during my designated "creative hours." As Pablo Picasso once remarked, "Without great solitude, no serious work is possible." This solitude became possible when I took control of my environment and set these boundaries.

I also silence my phone during work hours to ensure I'm not drawn into needless conversations or social media, which can fragment my focus. Informing everyone about when I will be free for questions or casual interactions has helped maintain these boundaries.

Lastly, and maybe most importantly, another crucial aspect of optimizing your environment is the people you surround yourself with. By changing the individuals in your personal life to those who are more in tune with your vision and more supportive of your goals, you can create a nurturing atmosphere that empowers you. Building relationships with people who uplift and inspire you can significantly enhance your personal and professional journey, helping you thrive in both areas.

Setting up an effective home office and creating a supportive work environment are crucial for maintaining productivity and fostering creativity. By establishing a dedicated workspace, setting clear boundaries, and optimizing your environment, you can create a setup that not only supports your business activities but also contributes to a healthy work-life balance. Remember, the environment you create is the foundation for the work you do. As Winston Churchill once said, "We shape our dwellings, and afterwards our dwellings shape us." This principle is especially true when your dwelling also serves as your workspace.

"You do not rise to the level of your goals. You fall to the level of your systems." James Clear

Chapter 6
Mastering Work-Life Integration

Achieving work-life harmony is a nuanced approach that differs significantly from the traditional idea of work-life balance. Rather than trying to allocate equal time to both work and personal life, work-life harmony involves finding a rhythm that integrates both seamlessly. This allows you to flow between responsibilities without the stress of constantly trying to balance them on a scale.

Achieving Work-Life Harmony

Work-life harmony acknowledges that the demands of your work and personal life will fluctuate. There are times when your business will require more attention, and other times, your personal life will need you more. The key is not to feel guilty about these shifts but to manage them in a way that does not cause neglect on either side over the long term.

One effective way to achieve this harmony is by keeping work confined to the office or your designated workspace. This strategy ensures that when you are in your personal space, you are fully present, allowing you to enjoy and value your personal time more. For instance, when I first began working from home, the lines between my personal and professional life were blurred. I found myself answering emails during family dinners and taking work calls during my supposed downtime. It wasn't until I made a conscious decision to confine work to my home office that I started to experience true harmony. I established strict office hours and communicated these to my team and family, ensuring everyone understood when I was and wasn't available for work-related discussions.

Strategies for Time Management and Prioritizing Responsibilities

Effective time management is critical in achieving work-life harmony. Here are some strategies that can help you manage your time better and prioritize your responsibilities:

1. **Set Clear Work Hours**: Define specific times when you are working and times when you are not. Stick to these times as much as possible to create a routine that everyone around you can also recognize and respect.

2. **Use a Planner**: Whether it's digital or paper, a planner is a great tool to visualize how you spend your time. Block out times for work tasks, personal activities, and rest. Seeing these blocks can help you make intentional decisions about how you use your time.

3. **Prioritize Tasks**: Not all tasks are created equal. Use the Eisenhower Box (a simple decision-making tool) to determine which tasks are urgent and important and should be done immediately, which are important but not urgent and can be scheduled for later, which are urgent but not important and can be delegated, and which are neither urgent nor important and should be dropped.

4. **Delegate**: Delegation is not just for the office. At home, sharing responsibilities can help prevent any one person from becoming too overwhelmed. This might mean asking for help with household chores or involving other family members in managing daily tasks.

5. **Learn to Say No**: Both in your personal and professional life, learn to decline requests that do not align with your current priorities or that could disrupt your work-life harmony. Saying no can be challenging but preserving your time for what truly matters is crucial to maintaining harmony.

Consider the story of Sarah, a small business owner and mother of two. When Sarah first launched her business, she found herself consumed by it, neglecting her health and family. It reached a point where her children remarked that she was always busy or distracted. This was a wake-up call for Sarah. She started by setting clear boundaries around her work hours and communicated these to her clients and family. She also began using a digital planner to block time specifically for family activities and personal care. Over time, these changes helped Sarah achieve a harmonious blend of work and personal life, leading to improved relationships and a more successful business.

Achieving work-life harmony is about making intentional choices about how you allocate your time and energy. It's about recognizing that while work is important, it should not overshadow the other vital aspects of your life. As James Clear, the author of Atomic Habits, wisely notes, "You do not rise to the level of your goals. You fall to the level of your systems." By establishing systems that promote work-life harmony, you ensure that both your personal and professional lives thrive.

"You can have everything in life you want, if you will just help enough other people get what they want." Zig Ziglar

Chapter 7
Building and Leveraging Networks

In the world of business, the old adage "It's not what you know, but who you know" holds a significant amount of truth. Networking and building a community are not just about expanding your social circle; they are strategic tools that can propel your business to new heights. This chapter explores the importance of networking, how to effectively build and nurture professional networks, and the undeniable impact these networks can have on your business success.

The Power of Networking and Community in Business Success

Networking is fundamental to business growth. It opens doors to new opportunities, provides access to valuable resources, and introduces you to potential mentors, partners, and clients. A strong network can offer support, advice, and guidance, which are invaluable in the entrepreneurial journey. As Helen Keller famously said, "Alone we can do so little; together we can do so much." This sentiment perfectly captures the essence of networking in business.

Engaging with your business community also enhances your visibility and credibility. When people know who you are and what you represent, they are more likely to trust you and do business with you. Networking isn't just about receiving; it's equally about giving. By supporting others, you build a reputation as a reliable and knowledgeable leader in your field.

How to Build, Grow, and Nurture Professional Networks

Building a robust network doesn't happen overnight. It requires strategy, effort, and genuine interest in mutual success. Here's how to start:

1. **Attend Industry Events**: Conferences, seminars, and workshops are excellent places to meet people who share your interests and challenges. Make it a point to attend these events regularly, engage in discussions, and exchange contact information.

2. **Leverage Social Media**: Platforms like LinkedIn, Twitter, and even Facebook offer vast opportunities for networking. Join groups related to your industry, participate in discussions, and connect with influencers and peers.

3. **Offer Value**: Networking is a two-way street. Think about how you can add value to others before asking for something in return. This could be in the form of sharing knowledge, providing a service, or connecting people within your own network.

4. **Follow Up**: After meeting someone new, follow up with a message or an email expressing your appreciation for the conversation. Keep the communication lines open by checking in periodically or sharing articles and events of mutual interest.

5. **Host Events**: Create your own networking opportunities by hosting webinars, workshops, or informal meet-ups. This not only positions you as a leader in your community but also deepens your connections with network members.

Through firsthand experiences in attending workshops, webinars, and in-person networking events, I have met numerous individuals who have significantly contributed to the growth of my professional network. Each interaction has provided an opportunity to exchange ideas and share resources. Many of these new connections have allowed me to email them with updates about the latest information, upcoming workshops, webinars, and summits. This has been instrumental in expanding my email list, allowing me to continuously market to an engaged audience and build trust over time. These interactions often open opportunities for these contacts to become future clients, further expanding my business reach and impact.

> Networking is about making connections and building enduring, mutually beneficial relationships. As Zig Ziglar beautifully put it, "You can have everything in life you want, if you will just help enough other people get what they want." By investing in your professional networks and community, you not only enhance your business's potential for success but also contribute to a vibrant ecosystem of collaborative growth. The more you connect with others, the more doors you open—not just for yourself, but for your business as well.

"An investment in knowledge pays the best interest."
Benjamin Franklin

Chapter 8
Financial Planning for the Future

Effective financial management is the backbone of any successful business. It ensures not only the sustainability of your enterprise but also supports its growth and expansion. While I am not a financial expert, my experiences have taught me invaluable lessons about the importance of sound financial planning and management. This chapter offers practical ideas on managing finances, budgeting, and planning for the future, aimed at helping you build a solid foundation for your business and personal finances.

Financial Management for Sustainability and Growth

Managing your finances effectively involves more than just keeping track of what comes in and goes out. It's about understanding your financial health and making strategic decisions that ensure long-term sustainability and facilitate growth. Here are some tips that have been instrumental in my journey:

1. **Understand Your Cash Flow**: Knowing how money moves into and out of your business is critical. Regularly review your cash flow statements to identify patterns, manage operational costs, and ensure that you have enough cash on hand to cover your obligations.

2. **Maintain Good Financial Records**: Keeping accurate and detailed records is not only essential for understanding the financial state of your business but also crucial for tax purposes. It helps you identify areas where you can cut costs and highlights opportunities for increasing revenue.

3. **Set Financial Goals**: Just as you set personal and business goals, you should also set specific financial goals. These could range from achieving a certain profit margin

to reducing overhead costs by a percentage. Having clear goals will give you something to strive for and help you stay on track.

4. **Plan for Taxes**: Tax planning is an essential part of financial management. Work with a tax professional to ensure that you are not only compliant but also taking advantage of all possible deductions and credits.

Ideas on Funding Strategies, Budgeting, and Financial Planning

When it comes to funding strategies, budgeting, and financial planning, being proactive can save you a lot of headaches down the road. Here's how you can approach these critical areas:

1. **Explore Different Funding Options**: Depending on the nature of your business, different funding options might be appropriate. These can include traditional bank loans, venture capital, angel investors, or even crowdfunding. Each option comes with its own set of advantages and challenges, so choose the one that best suits your business model and growth plans.

2. **Create a Realistic Budget**: A well-thought-out budget helps you control spending and assess your financial health. Start by reviewing your past expenses and revenue, then set a budget that supports your business goals while keeping expenses in check.

3. **Regularly Review Your Financial Plan**: The business environment is dynamic, and your financial plan should be too. Regular reviews will help you adjust to changes in the market or your business and ensure that your financial strategies remain relevant and effective.

In my own business, when I first started, managing finances seemed daunting. I quickly learned the importance of a good budget. Initially, I didn't account for irregular expenses, which led to some stressful moments. By the second year, I adjusted my budget to include a contingency fund, which smoothed out many financial bumps along the road.

> Benjamin Franklin once said, "An investment in knowledge pays the best interest." This is particularly true when it comes to financial management. Investing the time to understand and manage your finances can make a significant difference in the stability and growth of your business. Remember, good financial management is not just about keeping your business afloat—it's about setting the stage for long-term success and stability.

> "If your actions inspire others to dream more, learn more, do more and become more, you are a leader."
> John Quincy Adams

Chapter 9
Leadership and Empowerment

Leadership is a pivotal element in any successful business. It's not just about directing others but empowering yourself and your team to achieve collective goals. The most effective leaders understand that their approach can significantly impact their team's morale, productivity, and overall success. This chapter explores different leadership styles, how to choose the one that aligns with your personality and business objectives, and strategies for empowering both yourself and your team.

Exploring Different Leadership Styles

There are several leadership styles, each with its own set of characteristics and benefits. Understanding these can help you identify which style resonates with your personality and meets the needs of your business:

1. **Autocratic Leadership**: This style is characterized by individual control over all decisions with little input from team members. It can be effective in situations where fast decisions are necessary but might stifle creativity and employee satisfaction over time.

2. **Democratic Leadership**: Often considered one of the most effective styles, democratic leaders make decisions based on the input of each team member. This not only increases employee satisfaction and creativity but also helps the team feel more engaged and committed to projects.

3. **Transformational Leadership**: Transformational leaders inspire their team through effective communication and by creating a sense of commitment to a shared goal. They are known for their enthusiasm

and ability to motivate and innovate, which often leads to high productivity.

4. **Laissez-Faire Leadership**: This style involves a more hands-off approach, allowing employees to have a lot of autonomy in how they manage their workload. It can be effective when team members are highly skilled and motivated, but it might lead to poor productivity if they are not adequately directed.

5. **Servant Leadership**: Servant leaders put the needs of their team first and help people develop and perform as highly as possible. Instead of the traditional leadership model where the leader's focus is the thriving of their company or organizations, servant leadership inverts the norm and puts the focus on the growth and well-being of people in the team.

Through my experiences, I've learned that not all leadership styles will suit every situation, and often, a hybrid approach is best. For instance, when I launched my first business, I initially adopted a democratic style, which worked well until the business started to grow rapidly. I found that incorporating elements of transformational leadership, such as clearly articulating the company's vision and inspiring my team towards innovation, was incredibly effective in scaling up the business.

Ways to Empower Yourself and Your Team

Empowering yourself and your team starts with self-awareness. Leaders who understand their strengths and weaknesses are better equipped to foster a supportive and empowering environment. Here are some strategies to consider:

1. **Continuous Learning**: Commit to your own development as much as you commit to your team's. Attend workshops, read books, and seek feedback. The more you grow, the more your team will benefit from your leadership.

2. **Open Communication**: Create a culture where open communication is encouraged. Let your team know that their ideas and feedback are valued. This not only helps in solving problems more efficiently but also strengthens trust within the team.

3. **Recognize and Reward**: Acknowledge your team's efforts and achievements. Recognition can be a powerful motivator and can boost morale significantly.

4. **Delegate Effectively**: Delegation is not about offloading work you don't want to do; it's about empowering your team by entrusting them with meaningful tasks. This trust can boost their confidence and help develop their skills.

In one instance, a friend who leads a marketing firm faced significant challenges with team motivation. She realized that by stepping back and allowing her team more autonomy in how they approached projects, she empowered them to be more creative and take ownership of their work. This shift not only improved project outcomes but also enhanced team satisfaction and cohesion.

Effective leadership involves empowering yourself and your team. When I began to understand and apply delegation, not only did my stress levels decrease, but I also noticed a significant improvement in team morale and engagement. My team members were happier and felt more involved in the business because they had more opportunities to participate and contribute their skills and ideas.

This shift in my approach to leadership taught me an important lesson about flexibility in leadership styles. I quickly realized that adhering strictly to one leadership style was not conducive to my personal style or the needs of my team. Instead, I began to incorporate attributes from various leadership styles. This hybrid approach allowed me to adapt to different situations and team dynamics, ultimately leading to a more responsive and dynamic leadership model.

By empowering your team and allowing them to take on more responsibility, you foster a sense of ownership and accountability. This not only enhances their professional development but also contributes to the overall success of the business. Leaders who embrace flexibility in their leadership approach often find that they can respond more effectively to the changing needs of their business and team.

As more women enter the workforce in leadership positions, the leadership environment is becoming warmer, characterized by increased empathy and relationship building. This shift is not just beneficial for creating a supportive workplace; it's also great for business growth. Women leaders bring unique perspectives that foster collaboration, understanding, and a focus on well-being, which can lead to more innovative solutions and a stronger organizational culture.

This story underscores the importance of adapting leadership styles to fit the unique circumstances of your business environment. As you reflect on your own leadership journey, consider how blending different styles can enhance your ability to lead effectively. By embracing a flexible leadership approach, you set the stage for sustained growth, resilience, and fulfillment, not just for yourself but for your entire team.

Being a strong, empowered, and supportive leader is essential for leading your team to success. It's about finding a leadership style that resonates with you and adapting it to meet the needs of your business and team. Remember, as John Quincy Adams once said, "If your actions inspire others to dream more, learn more, do more and become more, you are a leader." By empowering yourself and your team, you set the stage for mutual success and ensure that your business is built on a foundation of shared achievement and respect.

"You must expect great things of yourself before you can do them." Michael Jordan

Chapter 10
Sustaining Growth and Pursuing New Horizons

Maintaining momentum and staying inspired are critical to the long-term success of any business. As an entrepreneur, your role evolves from doing everything yourself to leading a team that carries out your vision. This transition allows you to focus more on what you do best—being creative and strategic about the future of your business. This chapter will explore effective strategies for keeping the momentum going and planning for both your business's and your personal development.

Strategies for Maintaining Momentum and Staying Inspired

Maintaining momentum can be challenging, especially after the initial excitement of starting a new venture has faded. Here are strategies to keep you and your team motivated and inspired:

1. **Set Clear, Achievable Goals**: Keep your team focused and motivated by setting clear and achievable goals. Regularly celebrate these achievements, no matter how small, to keep everyone's spirits up and the momentum going.

2. **Stay Connected to Your Passion**: Remember why you started your business. Reconnecting with your original passion can reignite your enthusiasm and inspire your team. Sharing this passion regularly can also reinforce the team's commitment to the business's goals.

3. **Encourage Innovation**: Create an environment where new ideas are welcomed and rewarded. Encouraging your team to come forward with innovative solutions can bring new energy and inspiration to your projects.

4. **Keep Learning**: Industries evolve, and staying updated with the latest trends and technologies can provide new ideas and inspiration. Attend workshops, seminars, and other educational events to keep your knowledge fresh and applicable.

5. **Take Care of Yourself**: A burnt-out leader cannot inspire others. Ensure you manage your stress and maintain a healthy work-life balance to stay energized and focused.

Planning for Long-term Business Evolution and Personal Development

For your business to thrive long-term, strategic planning for its evolution is essential. Similarly, personal development must parallel the growth of your business to ensure you remain an effective leader.

1. **Develop a Scalable Business Model**: As your business grows, ensure that your business model can scale. This might mean streamlining operations, expanding into new markets, or continuously innovating your product line.

2. **Invest in Your Team**: Your team's growth is as important as your business's growth. Provide training and

development opportunities to enhance their skills and increase their value to your business.

3. **Plan for Succession**: Part of long-term planning is understanding that you might not always be at the helm. Planning for succession, whether it's promoting from within or bringing in external expertise, can ensure that your business thrives beyond your tenure.

4. **Reflect and Reassess**: Regularly take time to reflect on what's working and what isn't. Being flexible and willing to adapt your strategy is crucial as markets and industries change.

In my own journey, I realized the importance of focusing on what I do best after my business reached a certain point. I hired someone to help handle day-to-day operations, which freed me to explore new creative avenues for our services. This shift not only reinvigorated my passion but also brought fresh ideas that kept the business growing.

As you build a solid team and delegate day-to-day tasks, it's crucial to continue playing to your strengths—being the creative force behind your business. By staying inspired and planning for both your and your business's long-term development, you can ensure sustained growth and success. As Michael Jordan famously said, "You must expect great things of yourself before you can do them." By expecting and planning for greatness, you set yourself and your business on a path to achieve just that.

Conclusion

As we conclude our journey through "Thrive and Lead: Balancing Success and Fulfillment for Women Entrepreneurs," let's reflect on the powerful insights and practical strategies we've explored. This book is designed as a comprehensive guide to help you, the aspiring or established entrepreneur, navigate the complexities of business while fostering a fulfilling personal life.

Key Takeaways from the Book

Starting with a clear vision, we underscored its crucial role as the guiding star for your entrepreneurial journey. Strategic planning, tailored to align closely with your vision, helps transform your dreams into actionable steps. We delved into the importance of cultivating a resilient mindset, essential for navigating the ups and downs of business with grace and determination.

Skill development was emphasized as critical for staying relevant in a rapidly evolving market. We discussed creating a conducive work environment, especially for those who blend their living spaces with their workplaces, emphasizing the need for clear boundaries to maintain focus and productivity.

Networking and community building were highlighted as invaluable for personal and business growth, providing support, insights, and opportunities. Financial management was explored, giving you tools for thoughtful budgeting and strategic planning to ensure your business's longevity and prosperity.

Leadership emerged as a central theme, with a focus on empowering yourself and your team, ensuring that your growth as a leader parallels the growth of your enterprise. Finally, we discussed maintaining momentum and continually planning for both business evolution and personal development, ensuring that you remain innovative and proactive.

Encouraging Words to Motivate and Inspire

As you move from this book back into your daily life, carry with you the lessons learned and the stories shared. Apply them with courage and enthusiasm. The path of entrepreneurship is as challenging as it is rewarding, and while the road may be rocky, your growth, resilience, and fulfillment are interlinked steps towards your ultimate success.

Remember, growth is not just about financial gain but about expanding your knowledge and skills. Resilience will help you navigate through difficulties, and fulfillment will keep you motivated and satisfied with your life and work. These are not just goals but the very pillars upon which you can build a lasting and rewarding business.

As we reach the end of our journey through this book, I want to leave you with a story that I hope will inspire you as you forge your own path to success and fulfillment.

I started my own journey without a clear direction in mind, burdened not only by the physical toll of recovering from more than 23 surgeries but also by mental blocks filled with doubts about my worth and capabilities. These challenges often left me wondering if I was good enough to achieve the dreams I hadn't yet dared to dream.

However, through resilience and determination, I found the strength to heal both my body and mind. It was a transformative process, one that involved forming a clear vision of what I wanted my life to look like. This vision became the foundation upon which I began to rebuild myself and my future. I devised a strategic plan that would guide me not just in recovery but in life and business as well.

The journey of healing my mind and emotions was integral to my overall success. I worked diligently to rid myself of the negative thoughts that were holding me back, replacing them with affirmations and beliefs that empowered me. This mental and emotional clarity was crucial as it allowed me to focus fully on my goals without the weight of past doubts.

Creating an optimal working environment was another critical step. I organized a space that fostered productivity and creativity, which was essential for my next steps. Alongside improving my surroundings, I committed myself to further education. I immersed myself in learning everything I could about running a successful business, leadership, and coaching.

This education was not just formal but experiential, learning from every interaction, every setback, and every victory.

All these efforts culminated in the launch of a successful coaching business that allowed me to share my learned wisdom and strategies with others. Writing this book was a continuation of that goal—to reach and help millions of other women entrepreneurs who might be facing their own challenges and doubts.

This story, my story, is not just about overcoming obstacles, but about how anyone, with the right mindset, tools, and community, can turn their life around and achieve incredible things. It's a testament to the power of resilience, the importance of a supportive network, and the transformative impact of education and self-belief.

I hope my journey inspires you to take bold steps towards your dreams. Remember, it's not just about achieving success in business but also about finding fulfillment and joy in your personal life. As you close this book, may you feel equipped, inspired, and excited to start your own journey of growth, resilience, and fulfillment. Here's to your success, may you thrive and lead in every way possible.

As you close this book, consider it not as the end but as a catalyst for the next stage of your entrepreneurial journey. With the seeds of knowledge you now possess, go forth and cultivate a garden of success. May your endeavors be fruitful, your failures be lessons, and your life be a reflection of the balance and passion you aspire to. Remember, every day is a new opportunity to apply what you've learned and move one step closer to the business and life you dream of.

Next Steps to Thrive and Lead

Congratulations on completing Thrive and Lead: Balancing Success and Fulfillment for Women Entrepreneurs! Your journey is just beginning, and I'm excited to offer you exclusive bonuses that will propel you even further on your path to success.

- **Unlock Exclusive Insights**: Gain access to powerful tools and strategies that will enhance your business and personal growth.
- **Transform Your Approach**: Discover innovative methods tailored to help you overcome challenges and maximize your potential.
- **Stay Inspired**: Receive ongoing motivation and support to keep you engaged and focused on your goals.
- **Join a Thriving Community**: Connect with like-minded women entrepreneurs who are also committed to leading and thriving.

Go to **www.ThriveandLeadBonuses.com** now for exclusive bonuses and stay connected with all the amazing resources we have in store for you!

Made in the USA
Middletown, DE
15 October 2024

62747569R00056